A Pocket Guide to New Balance
May & Molyneux

A Pocket Guide to New Balance

May & Molyneux

Laurence King

Contents

Very few brands in the world of footwear have carved out a legacy as enduring and distinctive as New Balance. From its inception in 1906, as a small Boston-based arch support company, to its emergence as a global powerhouse in performance and lifestyle footwear, New Balance has consistently stood apart, not by following trends, but by setting them. This book is an exploration of New Balance's journey and the cultural moments that have cemented its status as one of the most influential brands in history.

At its heart, the story is of a balance between function and fashion, tradition and progress, athletic performance and everyday style. It is a journey that has allowed the brand to resonate with both marathon runners and casual wearers alike. Whether worn on the track or the city streets, New Balance shoes have become synonymous with quality.

This book is not just about shoes, but about the moments and choices that have defined New Balance's path. From pioneering technologies like the ENCAP midsole to the understated brilliance of the 990 series, each chapter explores how the brand has consistently pushed boundaries while remaining true to its core ethos. It is about how New Balance became a force embraced by subcultures, refusing to compromise on its values.

Through the pages ahead, you will delve into the people, products and pivotal moments that have defined New Balance's evolution. You will see how it found its place in marathons and music, on the feet of tech visionaries and global icons. Most importantly, you will discover how it has quietly but powerfully shaped the worlds of sport, fashion and culture for over a century.

This is the story of New Balance – its legacy, its impact and its future. A celebration of a brand that has never been just about footwear, but about moving forward, one step at a time.

The New Balance story begins in Boston, Massachusetts. William J. Riley (see pages 56–58) had recently emigrated from England in search of the American Dream, and in Boston he found a thriving industrial hub with a rich history in manufacturing, specifically in textiles and shoemaking. This in turn relied on a large workforce – men and women who spent long, uncomfortable hours on their feet. Riley saw the opportunity to make a difference and he founded the New Balance Arch Support Company in 1906 with the goal of revolutionizing footwear, focusing on arch supports. The name he chose encompassed his vision: innovative designs that would provide wearers with a 'new balance'. These early beginnings, marked by Riley's commitment to local manufacturing and customer satisfaction, shaped what would become New Balance's core values – authenticity, functionality and craftsmanship.

Riley's very first product was inspired by watching chickens run around in his backyard. He observed

RIGHT: The New Balance story begins in the USA.

8

how they achieved a perfect balance, supported on their three-pronged feet, and he proceeded to devise a flexible triangular arch support based on the same principle. Three support points were placed at the heel, the arch and the ball of the foot, and Riley proudly kept a chicken's foot on his desk to demonstrate the concept behind his invention to potential customers. His clients could also have their arch supports tailored to address their particular needs – a service that was unique at the time. The company soon established a reputation for its personal touch, while the products themselves provided welcome relief, enhancing the performance of shoes in a way that would lay the groundwork for the company's future success in the world of athletic footwear, where fit was so crucial to performance.

Riley's very first product was inspired by watching chickens run around in his backyard.

In 1927, Riley hired his first salesman, Arthur Hall (see page 58–59). Rather than sell New Balance Arch Support products via retail shops, Hall travelled the country selling them door to door. This personal approach was so effective that he was instrumental in broadening the company's reach. Nine years later, in 1936, Riley made him a partner. Then, two years after that, New Balance manufactured their first ever running shoe – spikes designed for a local running club called the Boston Brown Bag Harriers. These were made from kangaroo leather, a durable yet extremely light material for its time, and they quickly became popular.

During this period, the company continued to develop its commitment to improved performance and tailored solutions for individual needs. Then, in 1941, the company took what would later prove to be a significant step, expanding its product range with specialist footwear designed for other sports, including baseball and track and field.

New Beginnings

In 1956, the next generation took the helm, with the sale of the company to Arthur Hall's daughter and son-in law, Eleanor and Paul Kidd. At this time, New Balance was still a small team of employees producing products in-house, and relatively unknown. Although the Kidds continued to produce arch supports and orthopaedic shoes, they also began to transition increasingly towards the manufacture of specialized athletic footwear, forecasting the direction that the company would move in over the following decade.

The Trackster was released in 1960, four years into the Kiddss tenure, and its introduction was one of their most significant accomplishments (see pages 59–60). This was the world's first

ABOVE: The
Trackster.

running shoe to be offered in multiple widths, catering to the diverse needs of individual runners. At a time when athletic shoes came in a standard width, the Trackster was revolutionary. In addition, its ripple sole design provided better traction and cushioning, making it ideal for track athletes, long-distance runners and those who faced varying terrains and conditions. It was also the first New Balance shoe to cross a marathon finishing line.

Transformation into a Global Brand

On the day of the Boston Marathon, 17 April 1972, a young entrepreneur with a passion for running purchased New Balance from the Kidds for $100,000. The acquisition by Jim Davis (see pages 60–65) marked the start of a period of rapid growth and innovation, with the company evolving from a handful of employees producing only around 30 pairs of shoes a day into a global corporation employing thousands.

Davis suspected that the purchase would prove to be a great business opportunity, and he was right.

The running boom of the 1970s saw more people take up running for fitness and recreation than ever before, with an estimated 25 to 30 million Americans adopting the habit in just a decade. What had once been a niche sport for elite athletes suddenly became a mainstream phenomenon, with ordinary people realizing the benefits in terms of health, fitness and individual achievement. The streets began to fill with joggers; local road races and fun runs proliferated; running clubs formed; and marathon races (see pages 122–23) evolved into a popular and prestigious symbol of endurance and personal challenge.

> *Davis quickly set about taking the steps that would be needed to transform his modest new company into a major player.*

Davis wasn't the only one to see the commercial potential in this new wave of enthusiasm, so he quickly set about taking the steps that would be needed to transform his modest new company into a major player. From the start, though, he was also highly aware of the need to maintain the brand's hard-won reputation for excellence, built on its focus on high standards, customer service and customization. Under his leadership, New Balance continued to make shoes in different widths and place a strong emphasis on versatility, covering

ABOVE: Actress Susan Sarandon wearing New Balance in the 1970s.

RIGHT: New Balance SuperComp running shoes from 1978.

the needs of both amateur and professional runners and securing a broad customer base.

One of Davis's first moves was an overhaul of New Balance's product line, focusing on creating performance running shoes that could compete with the best in the industry. This led to the launch of the New Balance 320 in 1976, a shoe that marked a significant milestone for both the brand and the footwear industry as a whole, with its focus on superior performance (see pages 138–39). It was

also the first shoe to feature the now iconic N logo (see pages 32–37) , establishing a powerful brand identity.

Other models followed the success of the 320 – including the 420, a shoe designed with a focus on lightweight construction and breathability – and these formed part of a broader strategy to cater for all kinds of runners, from sprinters to long-distance athletes. New Balance's emphasis on fit, comfort and performance delivered across the board, making it a favourite among serious runners.

The New Balance 320 was the first to feature the now iconic N logo, establishing a powerful brand identity

Throughout the 1970s, New Balance refined its manufacturing processes and its operations, which was reflected in a significant growth in sales. The company's commitment to manufacturing in the United States was a key factor in its growth. Many competitors were outsourcing production to countries that were able to deliver at lower costs, but New Balance maintained its original focus on local manufacturing. This had always been a defining characteristic of the brand, crucial to building and maintaining a customer base that valued high-quality products.

By the end of the 1970s, New Balance had established itself as a major player in the athletic footwear market and began to release its first apparel products. The first of these were nylon vests, nylon tricot shorts, and shirts made from Gore-Tex, an innovative lightweight and waterproof material invented in the previous decade. Here, as with footwear, the focus was on innovation, quality and performance, and apparel was established as a part of the business that would only grow in the years to come. And when it came to shoes, running was not the only sport that New Balance had its sights on either. One example was its foray into tennis in 1979 with its first tennis-specific shoe, the CT300, which offered players responsive cushioning for greater comfort and traction on court.

An Expanding International Presence

The 1980s continued in a similar vein, with growth and innovation. The company released several iconic models during this decade that would come to define the brand, with perhaps the most notable being the New Balance 990 (see pages 139–42). First introduced in 1982, this was the company's response to a growing demand for high-performance running shoes. The 990 was designed to meet the needs of serious runners, but it was also a first for combining the very latest technology with premium materials. Positioned as one of the most advanced running shoes on the market, it took off straight away, despite the fact that it was also the most costly.

ABOVE: New
Balance 990v1.

During the 1980s, New Balance continued to expand
its product range too, introducing models purpose-
designed for specific sports. Basketball was already
dominated by the big players such as Nike and
Adidas, so it was natural that New Balance would
decide to compete in the same arena. In 1983, the
company introduced its first ever basketball shoe,
the New Balance Pride 480. It was designed to
provide the same level of support and stability that
had made its shoes successful with runners,
transferred to the court.

In 1984, a twenty-one-year-old Michael Jordan was
featured in *Life* magazine, ahead of the summer
Olympics that year in Los Angeles. The images were
taken by the Dutch photographer Jacobus 'Co'
Rentmeester. At the time, Jordan was a student at
the University of North Carolina; he'd not yet played
in the NBA and he'd not yet been contracted to Nike
(or any other brand). Rentmeester had just twenty

minutes to capture a striking visual, so he opted to shoot Jordan outdoors rather than on an indoor basketball court. Rentmeester had planned some shots with his assistant beforehand, taking Polaroids that he then showed to Jordan when he arrived. He wanted to capture the player in mid-air, as if defying gravity, so asked him to leap like a ballet dancer, with his legs split wide apart. The result was the now iconic image of Michael Jordan in flight, with a basketball in one hand and wearing a pair of New Balance shoes believed to be the Pride 480s. That same pose, with Nike sneakers replacing the New Balance, was later adopted by Nike as the Jumpman logo that advertises their Air Jordan range. It led to a legal battle in 2015 that Rentmeester fought and lost.

The world's finest made sneaker.

990

ABOVE: The 990 has become a classic. Advert from the 2020s.

In the 1980s, New Balance took steps to establish a stronger presence internationally. It began partnering with distributors and retailers to distribute its products across key European countries, where the appetite for running and fitness gear was now growing rapidly. This also involved expansion in terms of manufacturing. In 1982 a new factory was set up in Flimby, in the UK (see pages 79–81).

RIGHT: Dutch actor Rutger Hauer wearing New Balance in New York, 1980.

This move was aimed at addressing the growing demand from the European market and adhering to the commitment to local manufacturing that had already been established in the US, and it was noteworthy in an era when their competitors were shifting production lines to Asia. The investment in the UK appealed to a customer base that valued craftsmanship and ethical production practices. Shoes produced at Flimby were stamped with a 'Made in UK' label, which soon became synonymous with exceptional quality and heritage, significantly enhancing the brand's appeal in the European markets. The Flimby facility also had significant

practical advantages, allowing New Balance
to optimize their supply chain and minimize
delivery delays. Flimby became integral to New
Balance's European operations, and it produced
several of the company's most celebrated models,
including the 576 and 577, and the later 1500 series
(see page 147).

New Balance's expansion into Japan followed
along similar lines. It began at a time when
American culture and fashion was becoming
increasingly popular, so New Balance products
found a very receptive audience among the
Japanese, who also had an appreciation for
high-quality craftsmanship, superior materials
and performance. However, the brand first had
to contend with competition from home-grown
powerhouses such as ASICS and Mizuno. These
were companies with a deep understanding of the
preferences of Japanese consumers and they had

BELOW: New
Balance 576,
'Made in UK'.

long dominated the local sportswear market. New Balance positioned itself as a brand built on quality and cutting-edge design, offering a premium, timeless product. By collaborating with local distributors and retailers, it was able to ensure that its shoes entered the stores most likely to attract its ideal customers, thus securing a foothold in this competitive landscape. The brand's big breakthrough in the Japanese market came in 1984 with the release of the New Balance 1300. Sold at a very steep 39,000 yen ($130), the cost was justified by the premium nature of the shoe, marketed as the ultimate in running-shoe innovation.

Technological Innovation

Raising the bar for athletic footwear depended very much on technological developments, and in the 1990s, New Balance made significant advances, introducing several innovative features that set its products apart in the market. Particularly significant was the introduction of ROLLBAR technology (see page 96), a motion-control system designed to reduce foot movement and provide enhanced stability, particularly for those prone to pronation issues.

Another key piece of technology was ABZORB (see page 91), a cushioning foam compound that

RIGHT: New Balance expanded into Japan in the 1980s, and has been popular there ever since.

provided exceptional shock absorption. It was incorporated into the New Balance 999 in the mid-1990s, offering runners and other athletes a level of comfort and protection that was unmatched in the industry. The benefits were especially felt by long-distance runners, who looked for maximum cushioning to protect their joints and muscles over greater distances.

The 1990s also saw the launch of ENCAP technology (see pages 90-91), which used a core of soft cushioning made from ethylene-vinyl acetate (EVA) in the midsole together with a tough polyurethane rim for more support and durability – an optimal blend of cushioning and stability.

The introduction of new technologies was by no means restricted to the 1990s, and this topic is covered in more detail in Chapter 4, but this decade stands out as a striking showcase of New Balance's commitment to innovation and functionality, with each advance playing a crucial role in solidifying its reputation.

The Rise of Lifestyle Footwear

One of the major trends of the 21st century has been the emergence of a new category in fashion – athleisure wear. This hybrid style merges

LEFT: Runner Marcus O'Sullivan wearing New Balance in 1992.

performance sportswear with off-duty 'leisure' clothing, capitalizing on the technological advancements made in athletic wear to provide comfort and convenience for everyday purposes as well as exercise. With it has come the category of 'lifestyle shoes', designed to transition effortlessly between athletic wear and casual fashion.

New Balance's design ethos, which has always favoured simplicity over spectacle has made it a natural fit in this sector. Standout models have included the 574 and 990 – shoes initially crafted for running that have now transitioned into fashion essentials, celebrated for their timeless design, understated authencity and comfort. As a result, the brand now appeals to a consumer base that extends way beyond running enthusiasts, being seen just as often these days in images of fashion influencers and celebrities as on the sports field. Likewise, their versatility has meant that the shoes have found their way into high fashion while remaining accessible to those who simply appreciate well-made, reliable footwear.

To capitalize on this new direction, New Balance has reinforced its market presence through strategic collaborations with renowned fashion designers and labels (see pages 132–35). These partnerships have

RIGHT: Singer Rihanna wearing New Balance in 2014.

been key in cementing the company's status in the crossover space between athletic performance and mainstream fashion, maintaining its hallmark performance features while also catching the attention of fashion-forward consumers. Notable collaborations include those with designers like Todd Snyder and Ronnie Fieg, as well as with fashion houses such as Stüssy, Supreme and Stone Island, and they often feature unique reinterpretations of classic New Balance styles, incorporating modern design elements, new colourways and premium materials. The limited nature of each release creates a buzz and visibility for the brand, and demand among collectors and fashion enthusiasts is always high. Aligning itself with cutting-edge trends is also a strategy that helps New Balance pave the way to new audiences and position itself as a dynamic and forward-thinking player in the global fashion market.

New Balance, Today and Tomorrow

Like many others in the fashion industry, New Balance has felt the pressure to address the issue of sustainability, implementing various measures to minimize its environmental footprint, including the integration of sustainable materials such as recycled polyester and organic cotton. A particularly significant initiative has been the establishment of their 'Green Leaf Standard'. To qualify for this status, at least 50 per cent of a product, whether footwear or clothing, must come from an environmentally preferred source.

New Balance stands apart in the world of athletic footwear, preserving a tradition of domestic manufacturing that reflects its unwavering commitment to craftsmanship and heritage. New Balance proudly maintains a significant portion of its manufacturing in the United States and the United Kingdom. This dedication is more than a nod to its roots, it is a testament to the brand's values. Approximately 15 per cent of New Balance's global footwear production originates from its five factories across Massachusetts and Maine. These facilities produce more than 4 million pairs of shoes annually, with each shoe bearing the 'Made in USA' label crafted using at least 70 per cent domestic materials. This distinction not only upholds the brand's reputation for excellence but ensures the legacy of skilled craftsmanship continues to thrive

RIGHT: Model wearing New Balance at the Todd Snyder Spring/Summer 2017 New York fashion show.

on American soil. Across the Atlantic, the Flimby factory in Cumbria, England, accounts for around 5 per cent of global output. Known for its attention to detail, this facility produces the prestigious 'Made in UK' range. These models are cherished by collectors and style enthusiasts, and are a symbol of New Balance's ability to marry traditional techniques with contemporary design. Together, these domestic operations reflect a brand that values authenticity over shortcuts, demonstrating that in a rapidly changing world, New Balance remains firmly rooted in its principles.

Named one of the 'hottest brands in the world' on the 2024 Lyst Index, its future is well and truly assured.

New Balance is also committed to inclusivity and diversity, and has initiated several programmes aimed at enhancing representation and support for underrepresented groups within the sports and fashion worlds. This is a commitment that is also echoed in partnerships with a diverse array of athletes, and through campaigns promoting the importance of inclusivity and equality. Community engagement and social responsibility also receive attention, with support given to various charitable organizations and community initiatives, focusing particularly on those areas that are a natural fit with the brand – youth sports, education and health.

New Balance's evolution from a humble arch-support manufacturer focused on bespoke products to a renowned brand with a secure place in the global market is a story filled with significant milestones. Named one of the 'hottest brands in the world' on the 2024 Lyst Index, its future is well and truly assured. In a market where trends come and go, New Balance has managed to adapt thoughtfully, never losing sight of its identity and its desire for longevity. Its design philosophy is ultimately a testament to the power of restraint, creating products that resonate across generations and last far beyond the latest trends.

ABOVE: Many New Balance shoes are still proudly 'Made in the USA'.

Right from the beginning, New Balance was keen to establish a brand identity centred around quality and authenticity, and it's a strategy that has consistently differentiated it from other heavy hitters in the competitive sportswear market. It's a more minimalist approach that means its products are favoured by customers who value functionality and reliability over flashy marketing tactics, and who prefer footwear that doesn't seek attention. From its inception in the 1970s, the N logo has been a subtle yet instantly recognizable emblem of these same qualities. But how did this logo, so integral to the success of the company, actually come about?

The Iconic N Logo

In the mid-1970s, competitors like Nike and Adidas had already established themselves with their distinct swoosh and three stripes. These were not just design elements; they had become cultural signifiers, and New Balance was very aware of the need for a similar identity marker. Jim Davis wanted a logo that would complement the shoe without

RIGHT: New Balance logos ready to be sewn onto new sneakers.

overpowering it – he wanted the shoe's performance to do the talking. As he put it, 'We never wanted to be loud. The shoe worked for you, not the other way around.' The N was simple but effective, just like his company's approach to shoe manufacturing.

The person given the job of creating this iconic logo was Terry Heckler, a renowned graphic artist who had also worked on the famous Starbucks logo in 1971. Heckler's approach to logo design favoured simplicity above all else and the New Balance N proved to be no exception: a bold, blocky letter that would be easy to recognize from a distance yet would not dominate the overall aesthetic of the shoe. The letter N was chosen because it stood for New Balance, but it also encapsulated the brand values of neutrality and balance. As Heckler explained, 'The "N" had to be something that would fit with the product, not overshadow it. It had to reflect the functionality of the shoe.'

The first time the logo appeared was in 1976, on the New Balance 320 (see pages 138–39). Prior to this, the brand's shoes had been without a logo altogether, so the 320 represented not only a breakthrough in performance but also a milestone in the company's branding efforts. The timing of its debut was impeccable, landing right in the middle of the US running boom that had provided such a powerful impetus for the company. The 320 was praised for its performance, with *Runner's World* magazine naming it their choice for top running shoe, and its success propelled New Balance firmly into the spotlight. The 320 was not just a great running shoe, it became the foundation for the future of New Balance's branding strategy. It was appreciated for its understated elegance and it sat perfectly with the concept of high-quality performance footwear that had no need to rely on aggressive marketing tactics. In a market increasingly dominated by loud, attention-grabbing logos, New Balance's quiet alternative stood out precisely because it didn't try. It appealed to athletes who were serious about their gear and cared more about functionality than fashion.

As New Balance expanded globally, the N logo became a unifying symbol for the brand across various markets. By the late 1980s and into the 1990s, European consumers –

ABOVE: The N logo is simple but effective.

ABOVE: Limited edition Mount Fuji New Balance A09, made for the Japanese market.

particularly in fashion-forward cities like London, Paris and Berlin – embraced models such as the 574 and 990, which featured the N logo prominently. These shoes quickly became popular not only among runners but also on the fashion scene. The understated style of the shoes, along with the subtlety of the logo, were selling points, and they helped the brand straddle the line between performance footwear and casual street style long before the explosion of lifestyle footwear. The same was true in the United States, where both models gained traction in American streetwear culture, reinforcing New Balance's reputation as a brand that could deliver both functioning sportswear and fashionable everyday shoes. And in Japan, during the late 1990s and early 2000s, anything bearing the N logo became highly coveted, appreciated for its understated style and attention to detail.

Today, the logo endures as a symbol of the unique space that New Balance has managed to carve out for itself in the sportswear market. It stands in stark contrast to the over-commercialization of many other sportswear brands. Designed to be understated yet instantly recognizable, it has quietly asserted itself as one of the most enduring logos in the sportswear industry.

The NB Logo

The NB logo has grown into a fundamental part of New Balance's visual identity, working alongside the iconic N to represent the brand across various product lines.

The N logo is mostly found on footwear, whereas the NB motif has developed into a broader branding symbol, representing the company's complete range of offerings, including apparel and accessories as well as marketing materials. It was introduced in the late 1970s, when New Balance was looking to solidify its visual identity for a burgeoning global market. Once again, the graphic designer chosen for the job was Terry Heckler. His goal this time round was to create a logo that could embody the brand's ethos and provide a unified look across all product ranges, but with a focus on athletic performance in particular. The original logo therefore featured a stylized merging of the letters 'N' and 'B', with diagonal slashes cutting through them, evoking movement and speed.

The NB logo, like the N logo, has undergone subtle refinements over the years. In 2006, New Balance introduced one of the most significant updates to the NB logo as part of a larger brand refresh. The diagonal slashes within the logo were simplified to give it a cleaner, more modern look. This update also crucially made the logo more adaptable to digital platforms and various forms of media, enabling it to be reproduced easily across different contexts. The colour palette of the logo has evolved over time too. It was originally rendered in black and white, deliberately reflecting the brand's minimalist design principles, but, as New Balance expanded its product lines into different categories, it began to appear in various other shades, including red, black and silver. These new colour options allowed for some versatility, adapting to the specific requirements of performance gear and lifestyle products, without losing anything of the logo's impact or visibility. These evolutions have allowed the logo to perform its function, maintaining consistency across different product lines, while adapting to the diverse tastes of athletes, fashion enthusiasts and everyday consumers along the way.

RIGHT: The NB logo is used across a range of marketing materials.

Numbering System

A different Heckler – Arthur Heckler – left a subtle but transformative mark on the brand's identity. His creation of the iconic numbering system was a masterstroke of practicality and became a hallmark of the New Balance ethos. It offered a clear and logical way for customers to understand the shoes' unique features – be it width, support or cushioning – at a glance. Prefixes showed the intended activity, a model number represented the series, the last two numbers highlighted the shoe's primary function and suffix letters specified variations such as colourways or updated versions. By stripping away the need for emotive names, he ensured the focus remained on the quality and benefits of the product itself. This unassuming approach mirrored the brand's overarching philosophy of understated excellence.

Over the years, the numbering system has provided a sense of continuity and trust for loyal New Balance customers. It allows them to follow the evolution of their preferred models while helping new adopters find footwear tailored to their specific needs. Arthur Heckler's naming system transcended functionality and today his innovation continues to define the company's distinctive identity, standing as a quiet yet powerful testament to its enduring commitment to its customers.

LEFT: Model Heidi Klum wearing a New Balance T-shirt and shoes.

The Power of Grey

While most sportswear brands aim to capture
attention with bold, vibrant colours, one of the most
distinctive elements of New Balance's branding has
been its strong association with the colour grey. It
began with the release of the New Balance 990 in
1982, with the company introducing the shoe in an
unexpectedly muted grey colourway (see pages
139–142). It was a step in a very deliberate direction,
not just for its earthy aesthetic, but for the message it
conveyed. It signalled that the 990 was more than
just a high-performance running shoe; it was also a
versatile lifestyle product that could transition
seamlessly between athletic use and casual wear.
According to Joe Grondin, Business Unit Manager of

Global Collaborations and Energy at New Balance 2021–2023, the choice of grey was strategic: 'Grey was chosen because it fit the idea of performance meeting lifestyle. It wasn't loud or flashy, but it made a statement by not trying to make one.' The context of the market helped too – while other brands leaned into neon colours and eye-catching designs, New Balance's use of grey set it very much apart.

Following the success of the 990, grey became a core colour option – one that was especially popular in Japan and Europe, markets where New Balance shoes had found a footing on account of their understated appeal. The colourway has since been offered with many of its iconic shoes, including the 574, 997 and 1500, and similar options have featured regularly in high-profile collaborations with fashion designers and streetwear brands.

Today the colour provides a concise visual identity for the company, and it's used widely in campaigns and branding to emphasize its design values – products that blur the lines between performance and

ABOVE: Grey has been used across many different New Balance models.

lifestyle, that choose timelessness over trends, and that are built to last. This was formalized in 2018 with the introduction of 'Grey Day', an annual celebration of the brand's most iconic colour. Grey Day commemorates the part grey has played in shaping New Balance's identity and is marked by the limited-edition release of grey colourways of classic models like the 990, 574 and 997. Grey Day is more than a marketing event; it allows New Balance to honour its heritage while also reinforcing its stronghold in the current market. As the company itself has stated, 'Grey isn't just a colour. It's a symbol of who we are – boldly understated, quietly confident, and timelessly versatile.'

This is an understated approach to marketing and advertising that stands in stark contrast to the methods commonly employed by others in the industry. Where its competitors have tended to rely on celebrity endorsements, high-budget ads and trend-driven marketing, New Balance has, unsurprisingly, opted to go its own way, highlighting product quality, authenticity and innovation. Looking at its highly effective campaigns and taglines over the years highlights the success of that strategy.

RIGHT: Model Hailey Bieber wearing grey New Balance in 2022.

'Endorsed by No One' (late 1980s)

One of New Balance's most thought-provoking advertising campaigns, 'Endorsed by No One', launched at a time when the likes of Nike and Adidas were building their brands around high-profile athletes and celebrities. New Balance took a different path, and chose a slogan to match that would leave people in no doubt as to its stance. 'Endorsed by No One' was an explicit statement, and a clear rejection of celebrity-endorsed campaigns. New Balance's shoes, it was understood, were of such high quality that they needed no external validation. The product was the true star, not the celebrity wearing it.

'Endorsed by No One' was an explicit statement, and a clear rejection of celebrity-endorsed campaigns.

As the cultural landscape shifted, New Balance adapted its strategies without abandoning its core values. Rather than chasing fleeting fame, the brand partnered with individuals whose principles and stories aligned with its own. Figures like Jack Harlow and Jaden Smith embody creativity and individuality, while athletes like Sadio Mané and Bukayo Saka represent determination and excellence – qualities that mirror the ethos of New Balance itself. These collaborations did not mark a departure but rather an evolution, embracing partnerships that amplify shared values while staying true to the brand's legacy.

This delicate balance between heritage and modernity has allowed New Balance to remain relevant across generations. By blending its iconic independence with carefully chosen collaborations, the brand continues to inspire authenticity and trust, proving that evolution doesn't require sacrificing identity.

'Let's Make Excellent Happen' (2011)

A couple of decades later, New Balance introduced another campaign that put the focus on where it really mattered. 'Let's Make Excellent Happen' was designed to motivate people to reach their personal best. The campaign's message was rooted in New Balance's commitment to excellence in all aspects of life, not just on the sports field, and it aimed to inspire individuals to push at the physical – and mental – boundaries that stood in their way.

This marketing effort marked a significant turning point for New Balance on a practical level too, being rolled out through a combination of traditional and digital media, incorporating television, print ads, online and instore – a multichannel approach that aimed to reach a broad audience. The standout feature of the campaign was a television spot that was shot on New York's Pier 54, on a running track built specially for the purpose. It featured a select

handful of top athletes ('Team New Balance') captured in action on the track, showcasing how the brand's gear was integral to their performance.

The campaign came at a time when New Balance was launching some of its most innovative products. These included the New Balance 890 running shoe, featuring lightweight REVlite foam technology (see page 94), and the Minimus Trail, a minimalist, barefoot-inspired shoe designed for trail runners (see page 102). The advertising emphasized that New Balance's products were not just about style, but about helping athletes excel in their sport through innovative technology and design.

The campaign was also focused on building stronger connections with retailers, recognizing the rewards that had always come from its partnerships in this area. As Chris Quinn, who was New Balance's Executive Vice President of Sales and Retail at the time, put it, 'A major part of our success is directly related to our partners who own and manage New Balance stores. They're on the front lines making it happen and driving the consumer experience.'

The campaign was a success. By the end of 2011, New Balance had seen significant growth, with global sales reaching close to $2 billion –

LEFT: British athletes wearing
New Balance in 2012.

a 15 per cent increase on previous years. Inspiring visuals and storytelling helped to create an emotional connection with both athletes and casual consumers, reinforcing the idea that everyone had a right to 'make excellent happen', and that anything was possible with the right mindset and the right gear.

'Always in Beta' (2015)

Coming four years after 'Let's Make Excellent Happen', the 'Always in Beta' campaign was a major global initiative that focused on the brand's commitment to continuous improvement and innovation. 'Beta' is a term used in the software world to describe a product that is complete but still in need of refinement and testing before it's ready for release. The notion of having something at the beta development stage, in a state of perpetual refinement, was picked up by New Balance to represent a mission of relentless improvement.

This expansive campaign – far bigger than anything the company had done before – featured an international cast of 17 elite athletes, including the American middle-distance runners Jenny Simpson and Emma Coburn, British footballer Aaron Ramsey, German triathlete Sebastian Kienle, and representatives from the world of baseball – Venzuelan first baseman Miguel Cabrera and American-Dominican second baseman Robinson Canó. The cornerstone of the campaign was a

TV ad called 'The Storm', which showcased the athletes in a powerful narrative that followed a female runner overcoming mental and physical challenges across three continents. The ad illustrated a highly motivating message of resilience and constant progress, as the professional athletes, alongside a cast of amateurs, helped the runner, symbolizing a community of excellence. In the words of Rob DeMartini, President and CEO at the time, 'Always in Beta' embodied 'New Balance's commitment to never settling for past successes and constantly striving to improve.'

> *The notion of having something at the beta development stage was picked up by New Balance to represent a mission of relentless improvement.*

The campaign coincided with the launch of several key products, including the Vazee running footwear, which was designed for speed and responsiveness, and the 'Made for Movement' apparel collection, which, as the name suggested, was tailored for athletes looking for enhanced performance from their clothing. The campaign also provided the perfect springboard for New Balance's entry into the global football (soccer) market. The introduction of its first football products marked an important milestone in the company's expansion, paving the

ABOVE: Football player Marouane Fellaini in 2015.

way for it to apply its innovation-driven philosophy to a new sport, and to compete with competitors in a highly lucrative market.

As part of the campaign, New Balance also launched an immersive online experience called the 'Beta Hub' on its website. This platform allowed consumers to engage more deeply with the brand by learning about its athletes and product innovations via stories and behind-the-scenes content. This digital component helped extend the reach of the campaign and provided a way for fans to interact with the brand beyond traditional advertising.

'Fearlessly Independent Since 1906' (2018)

As a campaign designed to reinforce its unconventional core values, 'Fearlessly Independent Since 1906' couldn't have been more succinct. By referencing the company's inception and bringing its heritage to the fore, New Balance was able to highlight a constancy that had steered it successfully through more than a century in a demanding and ever-evolving industry. This was expressed in concrete terms by emphasizing its long-standing commitment to local manufacturing in the US and UK. It also involved a visual-identity refresh, with updated typography and iconography across all channels.

The campaign also featured an integrated 'Declare Your Independence' online campaign, featuring brand ambassadors that included Puerto Rican baseball shortstop Francisco Lindor and German football manager Jürgen Klopp, as well as the American athletes Rose

ABOVE: Baseball player Francisco Lindor in 2018.

Lavelle (soccer), Paul Rabil (lacrosse), Brenda Martinez (running) and the skateboarder PJ Ladd. Each ambassador was chosen for their embodiment of the independent spirit – all had a reputation for defying convention in their respective fields and staying true to their values. The campaign focused on highlighting their personal journeys, showcasing stories like Lindor's rise from a childhood in Puerto Rico, through the ranks of the American minor leagues, to eventually becoming a Major League star. New Balance partnered with major media companies like Vice and Bleacher Report to produce these documentary-style films and articles, and the stories of how each ambassador had overcome challenges and defied the expectations placed upon

them provided an effective amplification of the broader campaign's message.

'We Got Now' (2022)

'We Got Now' continued in a similar vein to previous campaigns, being built around the idea of encouraging viewers to take charge of the present and shape their own futures. In this case, however, the intention was to capture the attention of a younger, more socially conscious audience by using athletes and cultural figures known for their activism and contributions to society. New Balance underpinned its commitment to diversity with the inclusion of figures such as English footballer Raheem Sterling and performer and musician Jaden Smith (see pages 118–21), and the campaign resonated with the consumers it was intended to reach, with social media and an online presence playing a critical role in ensuring the brand remained relevant in a rapidly changing marketplace.

From its countercultural 'Endorsed by No One' campaign through to the progressive 'We Got Now' initiative, New Balance has managed to evolve as a brand, keeping pace with the times and maintaing a connection with successive generations of consumers, while remaining true to its roots: independence, quality and innovation.

LEFT: Football player Raheem Sterling in 2024.

The People

At the heart of New Balance's success are the people, from the leadership that steers the brand, to the designers, to the factory workers whose attention to detail ensures that every pair of shoes meets the highest standards possible. While the spotlight often falls on product innovation, performance technologies and marketing campaigns, this chapter redresses the balance somewhat by shining a light on some of the individuals who have kept New Balance running.

William J Riley

William J Riley was born in England in 1887, at a time of profound industrial and social transformation. The late 19th century was marked by intense economic growth in England, fuelled by the rapid expansion of factories, with the textile industry being one of the major players. This boom had created the sudden need for a substantial urban workforce, and it resulted in challenging living and working conditions for many. Perhaps this was something that Riley observed in his younger years, sowing the seeds

RIGHT: New Balance designer Stephanie Howard in 1996.

for his future vision. Arriving in Boston at the beginning of the 20th century he encountered another thriving manufacturing hub. With its textiles and shoemaking heritage, the city provided both inspiration and opportunities – the perfect backdrop for an ambitious innovator to develop his ideas and create practical solutions.

Arthur Hall

Appointed the company's first commissioned salesperson in 1927, Arthur Hall became a key figure in the brand's story. Prior to joining New Balance he had built a successful career as a travelling salesman, gaining extensive experience selling products across different regions. This background gave him an acute understanding of the importance of personal connections. His care for New Balance's clients went beyond the typical business transaction; he took the time to understand their needs, ensuring that the products he was selling would provide genuine benefits. This commitment to quality was central to his personal success, and it played a profound role in establishing the reputation ofRiley's company.

In 1934, when Hall joined Riley at the helm as a business partner, it marked a new chapter for New Balance, with Hall's business acumen providing the perfect complement to Riley's inventive spirit. From this point the solidity of the business was assured, laying firm foundations for the success that lay ahead. The next major step was a decision that ensured New Balance would remain in trusted hands through its next phase of growth – the sale of the company to Hall's daughter and her husband in 1956. Not only did the company remain within the family during this crucial transition, the sale also ensured that Hall's legacy would continue to shape New Balance's ethos into the future.

Eleanor and Paul Kidd

Growing up, Eleanor Hall Kidd had been surrounded by the world of New Balance. She had witnessed firsthand the growth of the company her father had worked tirelessly to build, and she had inherited the strong work ethic that defined his contribution. She also felt a deep sense of responsibility to continue what her father and Riley had begun, ensuring that the company remained true to its roots.

Growing up, Eleanor Hall Kidd had been surrounded by the world of New Balance.

Eleanor was actively involved in the business, not just a passive inheritor, and Paul was a man of strong character, known for his pragmatism and business know-how. Before joining New Balance, he had worked in sales and management, where he developed the skills necessary to help steer the company through the challenges of a growing market. Theirs was a solid partnership, both personally and professionally, with Eleanor deeply committed to maintaining the company's authenticity and family values, and Paul always looking for ways to grow the business. The Kidds didn't seek the limelight; they were content to let the product and their reputation for quality speak for themselves. When they handed the company over to Jim Davis in 1972, their decade of quiet leadership had laid the groundwork for the company's future growth. Davis would inherit a business with a strong ethos and a reputation based on performance, perfectly positioned to capitalize on the boom that was to come.

Jim Davis

Jim Davis is widely seen as the visionary who shaped New Balance. He was born in 1943, in Brookline, Massachusetts, to working-class Greek immigrant parents with a strong belief in education and perseverance. Davis learned about the value of hard work and self-reliance from an early age, and these values would go on to drive his business philosophy in adulthood.

Davis attended Middlebury College in Vermont, where he studied biology and chemistry. This

RIGHT: Jim Davis at the New Balance factory in 1995.

scientific background fostered a problem-solving mindset and a passion for innovation, both of which would later give him a critical edge when it came to product development. After graduation, Davis worked as a sales engineer, then a marketing manager, acquiring an understanding of market demands, customer service and business operations. Then, in the early 1970s, an opportunity came along that would change his life – he heard that Eleanor and Paul Kidd were looking to sell their company. At that time, New Balance was operating as a relatively obscure business in Boston, with just a handful of employees producing shoes in small quantities. Another entrepreneur might have passed on such a modest operation, but Davis saw immense potential. He purchased New Balance in 1972, on the day of the Boston Marathon – an auspicious start for a company destined to make its mark in the world of running – and he recognized that New Balance's great strength lay in its focus on fit and performance.

Davis believed in understanding every detail of how the company operated and made regular visits to the production facilities.

Davis's leadership style was distinctly hands-on. From the beginning, he immersed himself in all aspects of the business, from product design to manufacturing and marketing. He believed in understanding every detail of how the company operated and made regular visits to the production facilities. One of his most significant early decisions was his commitment to domestic manufacturing (see page 16). While many US companies were moving production overseas to lower costs, Davis was adamant that New Balance keep its manufacturing operations at home. This was as much about supporting local jobs as it was about a commitment to quality. His refusal to compromise on this principle became a hallmark of the company's identity and helped differentiate New Balance from its competitors at a key stage in its trajectory.

The values instilled in Davis by his parents, of integrity, hard work and respect, became the guiding principles of his leadership, but his wife also played an essential role. The couple had met while they were both young professionals – Anne was a businesswoman in her own right – and that set the tone of their partnership. Anne supported her husband's decision to purchase the company; she shared his vision and would go on to become an essential partner in its development. While he focused on product innovation and manufacturing, Anne brought a human-centred approach to the company's operations, focusing on philanthropic and corporate social responsibility as well as corporate culture and employee welfare, helping to build a loyal and motivated workforce.

Jim Davis's acquisition and leadership of New Balance did more than simply turn a small regional company into a major corporation. By focusing on the needs of serious runners and athletes, he created a niche for the company when many others were choosing to focus on style and marketing, establishing an enduring reputation for excellence.

Rob DeMartini

In April 2007 Rob DeMartini joined New Balance as its president and CEO. Likewise raised to have a strong work ethic, DeMartini graduated from San Diego State University and began his career at Procter & Gamble, where he worked for over 20 years, honing his leadership skills in managing iconic brands. He later joined Tyson Foods as Group Vice President, so he came to New Balance armed with a strong reputation in the world of consumer goods and a clear understanding of how to manage large-scale operations.

Under DeMartini's leadership, New Balance underwent a period of significant growth and strategic global expansion. During his 12-year tenure, New Balance's global revenue went from $1.5 to $4.2 billion, solidifying its place as one of the leading athletic footwear and apparel companies in

LEFT: Rob DeMartini in 2013.

ABOVE: Style-conscious New Balance sneakers from 2016.

the world. This remarkable growth was driven by a focus on expanding international sales, which grew from 30 to 65 per cent of total revenue. DeMartini's strategy was to tap into new consumer bases, increasing the company's reach in Asia and Europe, while maintaining a strong presence in North America.

DeMartini identified the growing influence of fashion, streetwear and youth culture and saw an opportunity to evolve New Balance's identity. While maintaining its heritage of quality and function, the brand began to weave style and design innovation into its DNA. Models like the 990v4 and 997S exemplified this shift, combining the technical

excellence New Balance was known for with a modern, trend-conscious aesthetic. This period also saw the brand form partnerships with creatives and athletes whose influence extended far beyond their respective fields, placing New Balance at the intersection of sport and culture.

DeMartini was also instrumental in positioning New Balance as a leader in the specialty running market, helping the company retain its status among serious runners and athletes. By prioritizing technology and product development, New Balance managed to gain market share from giants like Nike and Adidas, and its focus on performance running shoes in turn complemented the company's efforts to diversify its product lines, expanding into apparel, e-commerce and retail.

A cornerstone of his leadership was an unwavering commitment to 'Made in USA' manufacturing (see page 81). As his predecessor had also believed, doubling down on domestic production not only helped to ensure product quality but it also provided crucial support for American jobs. One of DeMartini's notable achievements in this area was advocating for the Berry Amendment, which requires the US Department of Defense to give preference to products that are produced domestically, particularly food and clothing.

Beyond manufacturing and sales growth, DeMartini established a strong corporate culture at New Balance. He emphasized collaboration and employee development, believing that a positive and engaged workforce was essential to maintaining a competitive edge, and his inclusive, hands-on leadership style created an environment where employees felt connected to the company's goals and values. Crucially, then, DeMartini scaled the company's operations without sacrificing the core values that made it unique. This approach not only helped build consumer trust but it also attracted top talent to the company. DeMartini stepped down in 2018, after 12 years of transformational leadership.

Joe Preston

Joe Preston succeeded Rob DeMartini as CEO in 2018. His career at New Balance had in fact begun way back in 1995, when he joined as a Senior Product Manager for Running and Lifestyle, and his two decades at the company in a variety of leadership roles had given him extensive experience across different areas of the business and a deep understanding of its operations.

Preston's personal and academic background is rooted in Massachusetts. He earned his bachelor's

ABOVE: Joe Preston (left) with Larry Lucchino (right), CEO of the Boston Red Sox.

degree from Merrimack College and later pursued an MBA from the business school Babson College. This business education, combined with his on-the-ground experience at New Balance, equipped him with the skills needed to lead a global company.

Preston took the reins just before COVID-19 and immediately faced a test of his leadership as the global retail landscape shifted. What seemed unfortunate timing, though, only demonstrated that he was the right man for the job. Under his guidance New Balance adapted quickly to the challenges of the pandemic, placing a stronger emphasis on e-commerce and expanding its digital platforms. It was a strategic pivot that not only allowed the company to weather the storm but in fact to see significant growth, with sales bouncing back by 29 per cent in 2021 after a 15 per cent drop the previous year.

Another important aspect of Preston's leadership has been his dedication to domestic manufacturing (see page 16), upholding New Balance's long-standing tradition of producing footwear in the US and UK. He has focused on making New Balance more sustainable, too, pushing for environmentally conscious practices across the company's operations. His approach clearly aligns with

RIGHT: Justin Bieber wearing New Balance in 2020.

the company's long-standing commitment to integrity and innovation, but it cannily also ensures that New Balance keeps pace with consumer attitudes, which are shifting increasingly towards products that are both sustainably and ethically produced.

Steven Smith

The evolution of New Balance has been influenced not just by its leadership but also by the creative minds that have shaped its footwear, dictating innovation and, ultimately, legacy. These designers have come from diverse backgrounds, and their combined efforts have carved out a reputation for performance, aesthetics and a responsiveness to the needs of the market.

Among the most influential of these designers was the 'Godfather of the Dad Shoe', Steven Smith, who

BELOW: New Balance 574.

created some of the most iconic models in the company's history, including the New Balance 574, 997 and 1500 (see pages 142–46, 147 and 148). Having been a runner at college, Smith began his career at New Balance in 1986, when he was one of just two designers at the company. During his tenure, Smith's creative vision reshaped New Balance's design ethos, with his contributions to the 99X series cementing his legacy as one of the industry's most influential designers.

Smith's first significant impact came with the New Balance 995, a model that married advanced technology with timeless aesthetics. The 995 introduced a lightweight design tailored for runners seeking both comfort and speed, setting the stage for a series of innovative breakthroughs. The 996 followed, further refining the balance between performance and style, showcasing Smith's ability to craft shoes that appealed to athletes and casual wearers alike.

However, it was the New Balance 997, launched in 1990, that became the crown jewel of Smith's contributions. Featuring the brand's groundbreaking ENCAP midsole technology, the 997 combined a soft EVA core with a durable polyurethane rim, delivering unparalleled stability and cushioning. Its sleek, modern silhouette broke new ground, proving that performance footwear could be both functional and visually striking. The use of premium materials and meticulous craftsmanship ensured the 997 resonated with a broader audience, bridging the gap between serious runners and fashion-forward consumers.

While Smith departed New Balance in the early 1990s, his influence continued to ripple through the brand. The 991, introduced in 2001, is often mistakenly attributed to Smith, though it was crafted by subsequent designers.

Tetsuya Shono

Tetsuya Shono's journey with New Balance began in 1997, when he joined the company in Japan with a vision to blend the brand's renowned performance ethos with an elevated design sensibility. Over the next two decades, Shono's career would see him rise to the role of Creative Director for New Balance Japan, where his innovative approach and dedication to detail cemented his reputation as one of the most influential figures in the company's history.

In his early years, Shono focused on integrating New Balance's core values into designs that resonated with Japanese consumers. His deep understanding of industrial design and functional aesthetics positioned him as a key player in New Balance's expansion in Japan, a market where precision and quality are paramount. By championing minimalist, refined silhouettes, Shono tapped into a cultural appreciation for

understated elegance, helping the brand establish a strong foothold in the region.

ABOVE: New Balance 2002R.

One of Shono's defining moments came with the reintroduction of the 2002R, a model that had originally debuted in 2010 as a premium running shoe (see pages 153–54). Under his creative direction, the 2002R was revitalized to bridge the gap between performance and lifestyle. This reimagining was pivotal in the brand's global resurgence, attracting a new generation of consumers while maintaining the loyalty of long-time fans. Shono's ability to preserve the model's heritage while making it relevant in the competitive sneaker market underscored his exceptional talent for storytelling through design.

Beyond individual models, Shono's influence shaped the broader narrative of New Balance in Japan. He prioritized craftsmanship and authenticity, aligning the brand's aesthetic with the cultural values of precision and integrity. His leadership not only enhanced the appeal of New Balance within the Japanese market but also inspired the global sneaker community.

Andrew Nyssen

Andrew Nyssen, a key figure in New Balance's design evolution, played a crucial role in shaping the brand's reputation for blending luxury with performance. Joining New Balance in the early 2000s, Nyssen was at the forefront of developing the premium New Balance 2002, a model that redefined high-end athletic footwear (see pages 153–54). His contributions dovetailed with those of Tetsuya Shono, who later reimagined the model as the 2002R, bringing it to a new generation of sneaker enthusiasts.

The original 2002, launched in 2010, was conceived as a statement piece, showcasing New Balance's commitment to innovation and craftsmanship. Nyssen led the design of its upper, taking inspiration from luxury automobiles and fine watchmaking, saying, 'I wanted to design a sneaker for our CEO at the time.' The 2002 was not only visually striking but also packed with advanced technologies, including the N–ergy cushioning system and Stability Web.

These features provided unparalleled shock absorption and support, with a price tag to match. Retailing at US$250, it was premium shoe, with a limited market.

While the 2002 initially catered to a niche audience, its influence laid the groundwork for subsequent reinterpretations. In 2020, Shono revitalized the model as the 2002R, introducing modern updates while maintaining its heritage-inspired essence. The collaboration between Nyssen's original vision and Shono's reinterpretation underscores the importance of teamwork and continuity in New Balance's design ethos.

> *Nyssen played a crucial role in shaping the brand's reputation for blending luxury with performance.*

Nyssen's broader contributions extended beyond individual models. His dedication to craftsmanship and his ability to merge performance with lifestyle appeal have helped position New Balance as a brand that bridges technical excellence with cultural relevance.

Joe Grondin

Joe Grondin joined New Balance in 2014 and was a driving force behind the brand's modern resurgence through strategic collaborations. As the Senior

Manager of Global Collaborations and Energy, Grondin steered New Balance into a new era, where partnerships breathed fresh life into iconic silhouettes such as the 990 series. His ability to bridge the gap between heritage and contemporary design has been pivotal in redefining the brand's presence in an increasingly competitive market.

Under Grondin's leadership, New Balance embarked on transformative collaborations with visionary creatives, such as Aimé Leon Dore, JJJJound and Stray Rats. These partnerships reimagined classic models, presenting them with a modern twist while staying true to the brand's values of quality and craftsmanship. The 990, for instance, was revitalized through limited-edition releases that married timeless design with modern aesthetics.

Grondin's focus on collaborations extended beyond design, positioning New Balance as a cultural touchstone. By aligning the brand with forward-thinking creatives, he expanded its appeal across diverse markets.

The People Behind the Factories

At the heart of this reputation for quality craftsmanship, of course, are the thousands of individuals who work tirelessly in its factories. While many global brands have moved production overseas, New Balance has remained committed to local manufacturing in the UK and the US (see pages

29–30), so it would be impossible to talk about the people of New Balance without highlighting those behind its sites on both sides of the Atlantic.

The Flimby factory in Cumbria's Lake District has been producing New Balance's 'Made in UK' line since it was established in 1982. It specializes in crafting some of the most iconic New Balance shoes,

ABOVE: New Balance 650 x Aimé Leon Dore.

RIGHT: Guillermina Burgos operates a stitching machine in a New Balance facility in Lawrence, Massachusetts.

including models from the 990 series, so it's an integral part of global operations. Many of the manufacturing processes carried out here, including cutting, stitching and assembly, require careful, skilled hands rather than machinery, with close attention paid to every detail. Unlike mass-produced shoes, the focus is on customization and small, meticulously crafted batches. The factory employs around 300 people, and for many of them, working at Flimby is more than just a job – it's a family tradition. There are many stories of different generations of the same family working side by side, passing traditional shoemaking techniques down through the years.

Products made under the 'Made in USA' umbrella are crafted at New Balance's two sites in Massachusetts (with its flagship facility in Lawrence), in addition to three more in Maine, and a sixth to come in New Hampshire. Together they employ well over a thousand employees. As at Flimby, work involves precise craftsmanship, whether it's sewing upper materials together or ensuring the perfect fit of each shoe, and the American operation has likewise seen different generations of the same families on its factory floors. This close-knit community atmosphere fosters a sense of responsibility, not just for the shoes they produce but for the environmental impact they leave behind. This is a core focus for both the UK and the US sites, with efforts made to use recycled materials where possible and minimize waste.

Local craftsmen have been the unsung heroes of New Balance since the beginning and the factories represent more than just production lines – they are powered by dedicated, skilled workers whose commitment to quality ensures that the brand's legacy of excellence continues with every pair of shoes.

Riley designed his original arch support to focus on the heel, arch and ball of the foot, distributing weight evenly to alleviate pressure and facilitate a natural gait. He was ahead of his time in recognizing that no two clients' feet are alike, and understanding that footwear needed to adapt to those differences to be truly effective. An emphasis on biomechanics and customized solutions has remained a central tenet for New Balance, even if the sophistication of technological advances over recent decades has superseded anything Riley could have foreseen.

The move away from orthopaedic products and into the world of athletic shoes continued under the Kidds' direction. With the introduction of the Trackster in 1960 (see page 84), they laid the groundwork for comfort and performance features that would characterize the brand's offerings from then on. As Jim Davis took over, an explosion of interest in running led to increased demand for products that could keep pace. Design innovations that addressed athletes' needs more effectively than those of its

RIGHT: A shoe being made at the Lawrence, Massachusetts, New Balance factory.

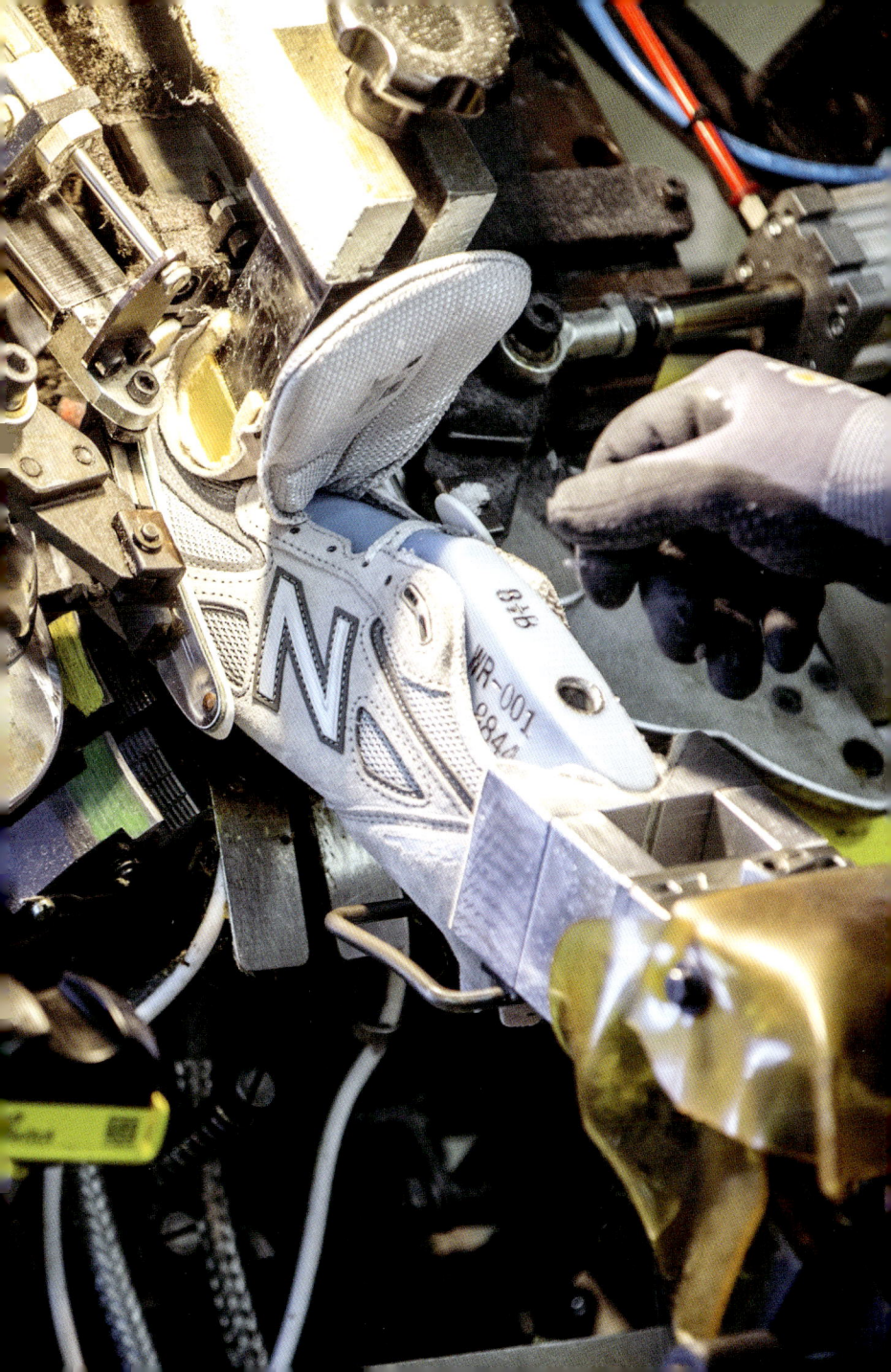

competitors helped New Balance establish itself as a brand focused on solutions.

Davis also saw the opportunity to expand into performance apparel. Athletes were not only looking for better shoes but also clothing that could withstand the rigours of training, so by the late 1970s New Balance had introduced its first line of sportswear, made from lightweight, moisture-wicking fabrics – in contrast to the heavy cotton garments that had dominated athletic wear previously. In addition to the physical challenges of running, athletes faced other barriers, such as weather, sweat and discomfort. Combining advanced footwear and performance-enhancing clothing was an advantage in the market, where competitors were slower to offer holistic solutions.

What remained at the core of the business, however, were the shoes. And as the business has evolved in the years since then, the focus on advanced performance has only intensified, taking advantage of new insights into biomechanics and evolving material technologies. The brand has continued to focus on core considerations that affect comfort and performance, such as customization, stability, cushioning, materials and propulsion.

The Trackster and the Ripple Sole

The ripple sole, which enhanced traction on various surfaces, made its debut in 1960 with the release of the Trackster. This model was the world's first shoe to feature a sole of this kind and it represented a huge step forward in traction technology. Replacing the traditionally flat sole seen on running shoes gave the Trackster improved grip on uneven or loose surfaces, making it popular among track athletes. A side benefit of the ripple sole was that it provided additional cushioning, making it an effective shock-absorber on hard surfaces. College track teams, including those from prestigious institutions such as Tufts University and the Massachusetts Institute of Technology (MIT), soon adopted the shoe. This early success was significant, not only in terms of sales but also for establishing the brand's reputation for performance footwear.

The ripple sole, which enhanced traction on various surfaces, made its debut in 1960 with the release of the Trackster.

Later Trackster models would refine the design of the ripple sole, addressing the issue of poor traction in earlier New Balance running shoes and offering stability and confidence to runners training in unpredictable environments and across diverse terrains.

Another innovative characteristic of the Trackster was its availability in multiple widths, addressing a

fundamental concern in footwear design: variation in foot shapes. The Trackster provided a more tailored fit, which led to improved comfort and performance.

Multiple Widths

Throughout the 1970s, the commitment to providing shoes in multiple widths remained one of New Balance's key differentiators, with Jim Davis continuing to push this forward, ensuring that the brand offered among the most comprehensive fit options on the market. This was a prime consideration for runners with feet that were wider or narrower than the average, who struggled to find shoes that provided a snug fit. Ill-fitting shoes would lead to discomfort, blisters and, sometimes, to injury or long-term damage. New Balance's emphasis on customization attracted a loyal base of athletes who needed more than a one-size-fits-all solution. The commitment to multiple widths continues to this day.

In 2005 the launch of the SL-1 last took customization to a new level with the introduction of a mould created to offer a more tailored fit for athletes with unique foot shapes. Developed from data-driven insights collected from a wide range of wearers, the SL-1 catered to varying foot widths and arch types, delivering an unprecedented level of customization

LEFT: Advert for New Balance shoes from the 1980s.

straight from the shelf. For runners with difficult-to-fit feet, this innovation provided a much more personalized feel.

The SL-1 is just one of many lasts developed by New Balance over the decades. For example, the PL-1 last prioritizes a slightly narrower fit for streamlined performance, while the OL-1 focuses on accommodating orthotics, offering enhanced support for those with specific medical or comfort needs. Each last is designed with a specific purpose in mind, reflecting New Balance's commitment to providing shoes tailored to diverse foot shapes and activities. Whether for everyday runners, professional athletes or walkers seeking comfort, New Balance's innovations in fit technology have reinforced its position as a brand synonymous with both performance and inclusivity.

Cushioning and Comfort

By the mid-1970s, as the running community continued to expand at a rapid pace, Jim Davis knew that in order to compete with the growing number of brands vying for attention, New Balance had to focus on solving the problem of impact-related injuries. Runners had long complained about the effects of running on hard surfaces, which could lead to shin splints, knee pain and even stress fractures. In 1976, New Balance introduced its dual-density midsole, a cushioning design comprising two layers of foam – a softer top

layer for comfort and a firmer bottom layer for stability. This allowed for better shock absorption, dispersing the impact on the foot and enabling runners to push themselves harder and longer.

In 1980, durability and comfort were improved with the introduction of polyurethane (PU) inserts. Placed in the heel and forefoot, these offered extra support and cushioning where the foot experienced the greatest impact. Runners, and especially those logging high mileages, often faced problems with shoes that wore down too quickly or failed to provide adequate protection against the repeated stress of pounding on hard surfaces. The PU inserts addressed this by offering a denser form of cushioning that not only improved comfort but also extended the lifespan of the shoe, ensuring it could withstand the rigours of daily training. This advancement played a crucial role in enhancing the durability of the 990 series (see pages 139–42), which became a favourite among long-distance runners.

In 1982, New Balance unveiled ENCAP, a technology designed to address the needs of runners covering long distances with footwear that could absorb the repetitive impact of running on hard surfaces without sacrificing support. ENCAP combined two key elements: a soft EVA foam core for cushioning, surrounded by a tough polyurethane rim that provided structural support. This combination delivered a shoe that felt soft underfoot yet maintained the durability and support needed

BELOW: New Balance 574, with ENCAP technology.

for extended wear. It was a critical innovation for reducing injuries due to overuse – a major concern for a growing population of distance runners. ENCAP became a defining feature in some of New Balance's most iconic models, including the 990 series, and helped the brand distinguish itself with a solution that catered to both comfort and stability – a balance that few competitors could achieve.

In 1994, New Balance introduced ABZORB, a technology that revolutionized the cushioning of running shoes for much greater shock absorption and energy return (the behaviour of a shoe as it recovers from compression). With repetitive motion over long distances, a runner's knee and hip joints experience the greatest impact and ABZORB cushioning was developed to counteract this with a unique blend of isoprene rubber and foam. ABZORB not only offered superior shock absorption, it also dispersed it evenly across the foot, minimizing stress at key pressure points. It also offered high durability because it didn't break down as quickly as traditional EVA foams. Runners reported reduced fatigue and discomfort over long distances and the technology became a staple feature across both running and walking shoes. It was later extended across various athletic and lifestyle lines.

Throughout the 1990s, New Balance continued to try and improve the weight and cushioning of its midsoles. One of the results was C-CAP, an EVA midsole technology that provided lightweight cushioning without compromising durability. EVA foam was already used for cushioning, but C-CAP took this a step further by using a compression-moulding process that allowed for better density control. By reducing the overall weight of the shoe, C-CAP helped athletes conserve energy, yet despite its lighter construction, C-CAP had the durability and resilience to withstand the impact of running on hard surfaces, making it a popular choice in shoes designed for both road and trail running.

N-ergy provided an added push, ensuring that each step felt lighter and more energized.

Building on the success of its ABZORB shock-absorption technology, New Balance launched a more advanced version in the early 2000s with ABZORB FL. This iteration incorporated a unique blend of Dupont Engage® and isoprene rubber, and it improved upon the original formula by providing even greater energy return and durability. Its ability to disperse impact made it a popular feature in a variety of New Balance models designed for high-impact sports, such as running and basketball. The technology played a crucial role in the New Balance 993, a popular model that combined ABZORB FL with other supportive technologies to offer superior comfort during long runs.

In 2006, New Balance unveiled N-ergy, a cushioning system that redefined how energy return and shock absorption were approached in performance footwear. N-ergy delivered an exceptional level of impact resistance and rebound, creating a spring-like effect that helped athletes conserve energy over long distances.

ABOVE: New Balance 530, with AZORB technology.

The core of N-ergy technology lay in its thermoplastic elastomer (TPE) materials, which provided the shoes with superior shock absorption while maintaining flexibility. Unlike traditional cushioning systems for absorbing impact, N-ergy provided an added push, ensuring that each step felt lighter and more energized, setting a new standard for responsiveness. The New Balance 1062 became one of the flagship models to feature it, offering runners enhanced performance during marathons and long training sessions.

ABOVE: New Balance 1500 with REVlite technology.

When REVlite arrived in 2011, it marked a turning point for lightweight performance footwear. New Balance created a foam compound that was 30 per cent lighter than traditional EVA materials. But this wasn't just about reducing weight – REVlite kept the same level of resilience and responsiveness as heavier materials, giving athletes the best of both worlds. Crafted through a compression-moulding process, it brought new energy to New Balance shoes. By offering superior shock absorption and energy return in a much lighter form, it became a favourite among athletes seeking that perfect balance between weight and performance, and models like the 890v2 gained traction as a result.

The introduction of Fresh Foam in 2014 continued the advancements in comfort and responsiveness. This cushioning system was the product of meticulous, data-driven design. Having analysed thousands of

runner profiles, studying pressure points and examining the mechanics of movement, New Balance crafted Fresh Foam as a single-piece midsole. With models like the Fresh Foam 1080, runners felt the difference. The shoe adjusted to the foot's movement, making long-distance runs smoother and less fatiguing. And Fresh Foam didn't just cushion – it reacted, responding to the runner's needs and changing how athletes approached long-distance running.

ABOVE: New Balance 1080 with Fresh Foam technology.

Stability

By 1978, New Balance had refined its midsole technology to address the need for greater stability during long-distance runs, and Davis and his team then turned to developing shoes that would provide a more seamless heel-to-toe transition, lessening the impact of a runner's strides. The outcome was the introduction of bevelled midsoles. The shoes of this era also featured flared heels, offering lateral stability on uneven surfaces. Runners could now push harder without worrying about their shoes slipping or tipping them off balance. With these enhancements, New Balance now offered shoes that were good for speed, while also helpful for those who needed extra support during long-distance training sessions.

ROLLBAR was designed to provide extra stability by preventing supination, supporting overall alignment and form.

The growth of running in the 1980s led to an increased demand for shoes that could fix issues with pronation and supination (a tendency for the foot to roll excessively to the inside or outside, respectively). In 1985, New Balance introduced ROLLBAR – a motion-control technology comprising a thermoplastic post in the midsole, designed to provide extra stability by preventing this rolling action, supporting overall alignment and form. This technology proved advantageous for runners with flat feet or high arches, who had a greater susceptibility to foot alignment issues and associated injuries. It also helped prevent plantar fasciitis and Achilles tendinitis, which often result from improper alignment. The New Balance 587 stood out as one of

the most popular models to showcase this
technology, quickly gaining popularity among both
runners and walkers. In 1995, New Balance refined
the system, now incorporating a thermoplastic
urethane post that ran through the heel and midfoot
sections of the shoe, creating a stabilizing platform.

In 1996, New Balance introduced the Stability Web,
a thermoplastic arch-support system designed to
enhance torsional stability while also allowing
natural movement. Positioned between the midfoot
and forefoot, it reinforced the arch to prevent over
flexing and twisting – common issues that could
lead to injury. Unlike traditional arch supports, which

ABOVE: New
Balance research
and development
team display new
models from 1995.

restricted movement, the Stability Web provided firm midfoot support while maintaining flexibility in the forefoot, ensuring a smooth, natural gait. It was also lightweight and durable, providing stability without adding bulk.

In 2010, New Balance returned once more to the issue of stability and motion control with the introduction of Stabilicore. Utilizing a post made from injection-moulded engineered thermoplastic, this was designed to reduce excessive inward rolling and provide arch support for a more stable platform. Runners found that it offered a more seamless transition from heel strike to toe-off, giving them the confidence to tackle long distances without worrying about the strain on their joints. It soon became a cornerstone in stability-focused models.

Materials

By the late 1970s, New Balance was already aware that the next leap forward in running footwear would come from material selection. Many running shoes previously had been made from leather, slowing athletes down with unnecessary weight, so the decision to move away from traditional materials was not just about aesthetics. This was a technical development that helped reduce foot fatigue over long distances and allowed runners to move faster and more freely while still reaping the benefits of the cushioning and support. This was particularly important for competitive runners, who needed every advantage when training and racing. New Balance began by incorporating nylon and suede into its designs, with the New Balance 320 (see pages 138–39) being one of the first models to benefit from the switch to lighter materials.

The next leap forward in running footwear would come from material selection.

By the late 1980s, New Balance had introduced ACTEVA, a new midsole foam that was 12 per cent lighter than the traditional EVA materials used in most running shoes, while retaining the same levels of cushioning and durability. ACTEVA was more resilient than earlier foams too, ensuring the shoe's performance and cushioning held up over long distances. By the end of the decade, it had become a staple in New Balance's lighter performance models. A significant advance in lightweight cushioning was then achieved with ACTEVA LITE in 2005, reducing the overall weight of the shoe. ACTEVA LITE's foam compound was 24 per cent lighter than traditional midsole materials. Through a compression-moulding process, New Balance tailored the material's density, ensuring flexibility in some areas and reinforcing support where it mattered most. Its impact was showcased in models like the New Balance 890, which became synonymous with speed and agility.

In 2007 New Balance introduced LIGHTNING DRY, an innovative fabric used for both performance apparel and footwear, keeping athletes dry and comfortable during intense activity. The fabric was designed to wick moisture away from the skin and allow it to evaporate, preventing the discomfort of sweat build-up – particularly important for long-distance running and endurance sports. By incorporating it into models like the New Balance 993 and various apparel lines, the brand extended its commitment to performance beyond shoes.

FantomFit produced a seamless, glove-like fit that moved with the foot.

FantomFit, introduced in 2013, reimagined how a shoe's upper should fit, using a no-sew overlay process to bond lightweight mesh with a thin synthetic layer. The result was a seamless, glove-like fit that moved with the foot, offering structure without the added bulk of traditional stitching. The technology provided a snug, flexible fit that adapted to the athlete's movements, which meant that the upper never felt restrictive. FantomFit also eliminated the risk of irritation caused by seams. In models like the New Balance 1600, the FantomFit design allowed runners to focus on their performance, knowing their shoes would stay comfortably in place, mile after mile.

ABOVE: New Balance 993, with Ndurance technology.

Durability

New Balance introduced the Ndurance rubber outsole in the 1990s to improve traction and durability, and it was further improved in the 2000s with the Ndurance Evolution, aimed to enhance the outsole's resistance to wear, specifically in high-impact regions, such as the heel and forefoot. The enhanced Ndurance compound was implemented in models designed for high mileage, providing athletes with the confidence that their shoes would hold up over long training periods. Providing improvements in durability without sacrificing flexibility, Ndurance Evolution played a crucial role in New Balance's high-performance running shoes throughout the decade, particularly with models like the New Balance 993 and 1064.

Propulsion

In 2013, New Balance offered runners the 'barefoot' running experience with the introduction of the Minimus range. With a low heel-to-toe drop – often as low as 4mm – the line encouraged a more natural running gait, promoting midfoot and forefoot strikes instead of traditional heel striking. Crafted with lightweight, flexible materials and Vibram outsoles, Minimus shoes allowed athletes to feel more connected to the ground while running, allowing their feet to move and strengthen; they were the ideal choice for those wanting to embrace the barefoot approach without sacrificing essential support.

Further innovation followed in 2018 with FuelCell, a nitrogen-infused midsole technology that transformed how athletes experienced energy return. FuelCell gave back, creating the sensation for a runner that the shoe was driving them forward with every stride, with models like the FuelCell Rebel

showcasing this new technology. The propulsion it provided made races feel faster, more efficient and less tiring. For runners looking to push their performance, FuelCell offered a tangible advantage – turning footwear into a tool for speed and endurance.

Recent years have seen the rise of carbon-plate technology, designed to deliver maximum propulsion. New Balance have embraced the trend, introducing a carbon-fibre plate into its high-performance running shoes in 2021. The carbon plate works in synergy with the midsole to stiffen the shoe, providing a springboard effect. Designed for marathon runners and elite athletes looking to shave crucial seconds off their race times, this technology helps reduce energy loss, enabling high speeds over long distances. The FuelCell RC Elite v2 became a standout model, combining the carbon plate with FuelCell foam to create one of the most advanced racing shoes New Balance has ever produced.

BELOW: New Balance FuelCell RC Elite v2 running shoes.

Over the decades, New Balance's pursuit of innovation has redefined the boundaries of performance. The brand has persisted in its mission to solve the real-world challenges faced by casual joggers and elite runners alike. Each advancement has showcased a clear understanding of biomechanics, material science and the needs of a diverse user base. It's also evident that New Balance's journey in technology is far from over, with each new breakthrough paving the way for future innovation.

ABOVE: Runner wearing FuelCell
SuperComp Trainer v2.

New Balance has undergone a remarkable transformation in its century-long history, expanding from a niche athletic footwear company into a cultural powerhouse that spans the worlds of fashion, technology, celebrity, music and sport. Its unassuming style, together with its reputation for quality and performance, has led to loyal fans from royalty to rockstars and among all age groups and interests.

The Dad Shoe

Practical, with comfortable thick soles and once worn by those who were considered too old to care about style anymore, the 'dad shoe' has had a comeback over recent years. When it was first launched in the 1980s as a performance running shoe, the 990 (see pages 139–42) was celebrated primarily for its technological advantages, but in the 2010s, this practical, unassuming design began to enjoy a new lease of life among fashion followers who embraced its chunky, utilitarian aesthetic. The dad shoe became a symbol of 'normcore fashion' –

RIGHT: Catherine, Princess of Wales, wearing New Balance in 2017.

PAGE 108: Actor Ben Affleck wearing New Balance 998 in 2015.

PAGE 109: Entrepreneur Steve Jobs wearing New Balance 992 in 2003.

celebrating simplicity and practicality rather than chasing trends. As the trend gained momentum, sneaker heads were not the only ones with the shoes on their feet; as the New Balance slogan put it, this was a shoe 'worn by supermodels in London and dads in Ohio'. Its blend of retro aesthetics and functionality allowed the 990 series to thrive at a time when fashion had begun to turn away from the fleeting and the disposable, seeking authenticity and heritage instead.

One of the most influential people to exemplify the normcore look was Steve Jobs, whose signature work uniform was an understated combination of black turtleneck, jeans and a pair of grey New Balance 992s. His go-to sneakers, released in 2006, soon became as iconic as the products he unveiled while wearing them. The impact was immediate. Jobs's regular appearances in the 992s helped to elevate New Balance's profile within the tech community and beyond, sending the message that the brand's footwear was not just for athletes, it was also perfect for those who valued functionality and design. The shoes became a symbol of innovation and tech-forward thinking, and their understated style led them away from the running track and into Silicon Valley and boardrooms around the world.

RIGHT: Former US President, Bill Clinton, wearing New Balance 1500 in 1994.

Back in the 1990s another high-profile figure from an entirely different world had a similar impact. During his presidency, Bill Clinton was known for his dedication to maintaining a regular fitness routine despite his schedule, and he was often photographed out jogging. Some of the most iconic shots of the time capture him in the grounds of the White House or on Washington's National Mall wearing New Balance shoes – often a pair of grey 1500s (see page 147). The photos worked in his favour, evidence of his dedication and down-to-earth nature, and they boosted New Balance's profile at the same time. Even if you were a busy world leader squeezing in a run between meetings, New Balance was the brand you turned to. Sales soared as a result.

Music

Back in the 1980s, New Balance shoes began appearing on the urban music scene, with their comfortable, easy style proving a natural fit with hip-hop style. The trend has surged in the 21st century, with US rappers Raekwon and Nas embracing New Balance, further entwining the brand with street style, especially through models like the 574 and 990 (see pages 139–45).

New Balance also found an audience that appreciated its blend of form and function in the worlds of grunge and indie music. The 1990s saw a surge in appreciation for New Balance among alternative musicians and their fans, who embraced the brand's lack of flash. Unlike some of the companies that leaned into the grunge trend, New Balance maintained its straightforward approach, inadvertently resonating with those who saw style as a personal statement rather than a fashion-driven look.

By joining forces with some of the most progressive names in the business via a series of high-profile collaborations, the brand has cemented its connection with artists in the music industry, and this has naturally trickled down to their fans.

The 1990s saw a surge in appreciation for New Balance among alternative musicians and their fans, who embraced the brand's lack of flash.

Action Bronson, the larger-than-life rapper, chef and television personality, has long been associated with New Balance, thanks to his personal affinity for the brand. Starting in the early 2010s, Bronson became a vocal champion of New Balance sneakers, frequently referencing them in interviews, wearing them in performances, and showcasing them across his social media platforms. His genuine appreciation for the brand, rooted in their quality and understated style, made him a natural yet unofficial ambassador.

This longstanding relationship culminated in a
formal partnership in 2023, when New Balance
announced its first official collaboration with
Bronson. The debut project, the New Balance 990v6
'Baklava', was a reflection of Bronson's eclectic
personality and creative vision. Designed with bold
colourways and unique textures, the shoe was a
celebration of individuality, blending New Balance's
premium craftsmanship with Bronson's flair for the

unconventional. The collaboration's success not only marked a new chapter for the brand – but also solidified Bronson's role as a cultural bridge between New Balance and a new generation of fans.

The journey from organic fan to official collaborator speaks volumes about Bronson's influence and New Balance's appreciation for authenticity. Their partnership exemplifies how a shared ethos and genuine admiration can evolve into a collaboration that redefines the boundaries of performance, style and cultural relevance.

Jack Harlow, the renowned rapper and singer, also cultivated a natural synergy with New Balance that began long before his official partnership. In 2020, Harlow subtly showcased his affinity for the brand in the music video for his hit single 'Tyler Herro' (a tribute to the basketball player of the same name), where New Balance sneakers featured prominently. This understated nod to the brand captured the attention of fans and marked the beginning of a connection that felt both organic and authentic.

By February 2022, this informal association evolved into an official ambassadorship, with Harlow joining New Balance's list of cultural collaborators. Known for his effortless charm and relatable style, Harlow embodied the brand's ethos of quiet confidence and timeless appeal. His laid-back aesthetic resonated

deeply with younger audiences, further bridging the gap between performance footwear and everyday fashion.

In October 2024, Harlow elevated his partnership by contributing to New Balance's product line with the release of the 1906R 'Rose Runner'. This floral pink-and-green reimagining of the 1906R – a silhouette originally introduced in 2010 – merged the brand's commitment to innovation with Harlow's modern sensibility. The collaboration highlighted New Balance's ability to maintain its heritage while appealing to a contemporary audience.

Meanwhile, the critically acclaimed north London rapper and actress Little Simz has given New Balance an entree into the UK's flourishing grime and streetwear scene. Once again, it has been the revival of a classic shoe that has led the way. In this case it was the chunky 878 from the 1990s; it was updated and re-released in 2021, in this latest iteration in a grey colourway. This collaboration represented more than just product promotion, it reflected the shared values of creativity. Little Simz's rise in the UK music scene coincided with New Balance's growing appeal in UK street culture, where shoes like the 550 and 990 had become staples among fashion-forward consumers.

LEFT: Musician Jack Harlow wearing New Balance in 2022.

One of the most high-profile associations of recent years has been with the actor and music artist Jaden Smith, which has propelled the brand even further into the youth and streetwear markets, along with an equally significant emphasis on environmentally responsible practices. Known for his bold fashion choices and his activism, Jaden Smith has been an ambassador for the brand for several years now, bringing a unique perspective to the table. The first collaboration was 2020's Vision Racer 'ReWorked', a sneaker that combined bold design elements with 30 per cent textile offcuts (and formed part of the broader Green Leaf initiative). The eco-conscious construction of the shoe spoke directly to Smith's generation, being a sustainable offering that didn't sacrifice style. This partnership wasn't just about aesthetics, but about changing

RIGHT: Musician Little Simz wearing New Balance in 2021.

ABOVE: Jaden Smith
x Vision Racer.

the conversation around fashion's impact on the environment. Released just in time for Earth Day, the Vision Racer 'ReWorked' became a statement shoe, celebrated not just for its look but for its message. Smith has since followed up with several other collaborations, including a new release of the 574 in 2022, and the launch of the 0.01 in 2023, with a follow-up 'Panda' colourway of the same shoe the following year.

Although recent headlines have often tended to be focused on the inroads New Balance has made in the world of music and street culture, its long-standing associations with the sporting world have continued, with perhaps one of the most enduring being its relationship with marathon culture.

LEFT: Actor and musician Jaden Smith
wearing New Balance in 2018.

Marathons

New Balance's history with marathons begins, fittingly, in Boston – home to the world's oldest annual marathon. Although not the official sponsor, there has been a strong association with the race since the company first launched in 1906. The brand continues to use the marathon as a platform, showcasing its latest technologies, releasing limited-edition Boston-themed products, including the highly sought-after Fresh Foam models (see pages 94–95), and hosting pop-up shops and community events that celebrate the sport's rich history in the city in the lead-up to the race. In 2017, for example, the 'This is Boston' campaign paid tribute to local icons from the worlds of running, hockey, baseball and basketball.

New Balance has, however, been the official clothing and footwear sponsor of the London Marathon since 2018. The deal established its presence at one of the seven prestigious marathon races that together form the World Marathon Majors – the others being Boston, Tokyo, Sydney, Berlin, Chicago and New York. The London Marathon is renowned for its mix of elite competition and amateur participation, making it an ideal fit for New Balance, which prides itself on catering to both top-tier athletes and everyday runners. New Balance provides footwear and apparel for its competitors and volunteers, releasing limited-edition London Marathon collections every year that combine their performance technology with commemorative designs. The marathon has been used to spotlight several of its newest innovations, from FuelCell midsole technology to Fresh Foam cushioning, underpinning its legacy in the world of long-distance running.

The London Marathon is renowned for its mix of elite competition and amateur participation, making it an ideal fit for New Balance,

New Balance has also been the official sponsor of the New York Road Runners since 2017 – one of the largest running organizations in the US and host to the New York City Marathon – in a deal that involves providing apparel and footwear in addition to a range of other initiatives, such as community events and programmes designed to attract younger runners to the sport. The brand have various other sponsorship deals in place too, with races at both the regional and international level, in countries including Japan, Germany and France.

Basketball

New Balance's journey in basketball has been defined by its unique approach to performance and style. Models like the PRIDE 480, from the 1980s, showcased the brand's commitment to crafting reliable basketball shoes, while modern releases have brought cutting-edge innovation to the sport.

Long before its recent resurgence, New Balance had a brush with basketball immortality. Michael Jordan, then a rising star, famously wore New Balance sneakers during his 'Jumpman' shot, an iconic moment that would later become a symbol of basketball greatness (see page 19). While New Balance's relationship with basketball has evolved over the years, this early association underscored New Balance's quiet but impactful presence in basketball's narrative.

In 2018, New Balance made the move to re-enter the basketball market by signing one of the NBA's most powerful players, Kawhi Leonard. Taking on the brands that were already dominating this market was no small matter, since New Balance hadn't been active in basketball endorsements for decades, but Leonard's reputation as a reserved yet fierce competitor was the perfect match for the brand's understated, performance-driven ethos. Leonard's endorsement led to the creation of a series of KAWHI styles, performance basketball shoes designed to match his versatile playing style. The shoes quickly gained popularity among fans

RIGHT: Basketball player Kawhi Leonard wearing New Balance in 2020.

and players. The endorsement deal also came at a conveniently pivotal time in Leonard's career, just before he led the Toronto Raptors to their first-ever NBA championship in 2019. His success on the court and his persona, combined with New Balance's sleek marketing, brought positive attention to the brand and solidified their credibility in the sport.

Skateboarding

New Balance's popularity within the skateboarding community further highlights its diverse appeal. It wasn't an association that existed in the brand's earlier days, but the shoes' durability, impact absorption and grip earned them a place in the sport once skaters began to explore models beyond the traditional skate-specific brands. This was made official when New Balance launched its Numeric line in 2013, which directly catered to skaters.

Central to Numeric's success has been its collaboration with prominent figures in the skateboarding community. Notably, professional skateboarder PJ Ladd became a key ambassador for the line, bringing authenticity to New Balance's skateboarding endeavours. Ladd's involvement, along with other esteemed skaters, has solidified Numeric's standing within the skate community, demonstrating New Balance's dedication to producing high-quality, performance-oriented skate shoes.

Football

In 2015 New Balance announced its intention to enter the world of association football (or soccer) and it has since become one of the sport's most prominent brands, aided by the strategic sponsorship of players whose reputations resonate with the brand's image.

ABOVE:
Skateboarder
Alexis Sablone
wearing New
Balance in 2018.

One of these is Senegal-born Sadio Mané, who signed with UK Premier League club Liverpool in 2016 for a reported £34 million, making history as the most expensive African player to date. He took up New Balance sponsorship in 2018. As a world-class athlete, Mané brings credibility to New Balance's performance-oriented focus, but his

RIGHT: Football player Bukayo Saka in 2024.

reputation for authenticity and giving back
reinforces a connection with fans who value
his character as much as his talent.

The English football star Bukayo Saka – a standout
player for Arsenal and the England national team –
signed with New Balance in 2021 when he was still a

LEFT: Football
player Sadio
Mané in 2022.

teenager. His sponsorship symbolized the brand's desire to align itself with young talent, and Saka brought the right blend of commitment, resilience and potential. His influence in the football world has allowed New Balance to tap into a younger, sport-centric demographic, especially those inspired by his dedication, humility and sense of fair play.

Fashion

New Balance's success with style tribes that otherwise have little in common has been one of the most interesting aspects of this journey, fuelled by the brand's adaptable aesthetic. One of the more notable of these was the UK football casuals subculture. Originating in the late 1970s, this trend arose among young male football fans who began to reject traditional fan attire in favour of designer sportswear brands such as Fred Perry, Lacoste and Fila. And to distinguish themselves from wearers of more traditional sneaker brands, many began to choose New Balance. Models like the 576 and 1500 (see page 174), in particular, were cornerstones of casual culture until well into the 2010s, valued for their understated heritage appeal.

Not long after the rise of the football casuals, the brand began to take off in Japan, cemented with the success of the exclusive New Balance 1300 in

RIGHT: Guest at Tokyo Fashion Week 2018 wearing New Balance.

1984. Here, the brand's 'all American' appeal was a hit with streetwear enthusiasts who also had an eye for detail and craftsmanship. New Balance became a premium choice, chosen not just for functionality but as high-fashion streetwear. Japanese designers and cultural influencers celebrated the brand's heritage models, particularly the 990 series, for their minimalist design and superior build, helping to establish New Balance as a lasting staple of Japanese street fashion.

In 2018, New Balance established their Tokyo Design Studio (TDS) to cater to the sophisticated and highly discerning Japanese market. With a deep commitment to detail and an emphasis on quality craftsmanship, the studio's designs have elevated New Balance's offerings, creating a bridge between technical innovation and high fashion. The influence of TDS extends beyond Japan, feeding back into Western markets where New Balance's elevated designs have gained traction within the streetwear and lifestyle landscapes. Japanese sneaker culture, revered for its appreciation of craftsmanship and minimalist design, has significantly influenced the way New Balance is perceived globally. TDS has become a key driver in positioning New Balance as a brand capable of delivering both technical excellence and cultural relevance.

In recent years, New Balance has strategically partnered with various brands and designers to reinterpret its classic silhouettes, infusing them with fresh perspectives and allowing them to reach new markets within streetwear and fashion. These collaborations have allowed New Balance to explore new design territories while honouring its rich heritage, appealing to a diverse and fashion-forward audience.

New Balance established their Tokyo Design Studio to cater to the sophisticated and highly discerning Japanese market.

Since 2019, New Balance has collaborated with New York-based fashion label Aimé Leon Dore (ALD) on several projects. Notably, the partnership revived the 550 silhouette, transforming it into a cultural staple (see page 145). The collaboration also included models like the 997 (see page 148) and 990v2, featuring vintage-inspired details and premium materials, blending New Balance's heritage with ALD's contemporary design ethos.

Renowned designer Salehe Bembury has partnered with New Balance on multiple occasions, bringing bold, nature-inspired elements to classic models. In 2020, the collaboration introduced the 2002R 'Peace Be the Journey', featuring earthy tones and unique materials. In 2024, Bembury reimagined the 991v2 with a vibrant purple suede upper and contrasting

accents, showcasing his distinctive design approach. In 2021, New Balance and Italian luxury brand Stone Island collaborated to release the RC Elite V2, a performance running shoe that combined Stone Island's innovative materials with New Balance's athletic expertise. This partnership continued in 2022 with the launch of the FuelCell C_1, featuring advanced cushioning technology and a distinctive design. In 2023, the collaboration expanded to include the 574 Legacy and 991v2 models, showcasing a blend of heritage aesthetics and modern functionality.

Amsterdam-based streetwear label Patta teamed up with New Balance in 2021 to celebrate the twentieth anniversary of the 991 silhouette. The collaboration resulted in the 'Peach Grey' 991, featuring a breathable grey mesh and burnt-pink suede upper, with cream leather accents and Patta embroidery on the ankle. This release highlighted Patta's ability to infuse classic models with contemporary flair.

In 2022, New Balance partnered with Italian luxury fashion house Miu Miu to reinterpret the 574 silhouette (see pages 142–45). Miu Miu introduced distressed detailing and raw-edged denim uppers, merging rugged functionality with high-fashion sensibilities. The collaboration continued in 2024 with the release of the 530 model in premium leather, available in black and white colourways, further blending luxury aesthetics with athletic design.

In 2024, New Balance collaborated with Italian luxury brand Loro Piana to create an ultra-premium iteration of the 990v6 model. This sneaker featured Loro Piana's signature Pecora Nera wool, sourced from dark merino sheep in New Zealand, and was priced at $1,500. The design showcased evergreen neutrals with deep red accents, combining New Balance's craftsmanship with Loro Piana's luxurious materials.

New Balance's design philosophy has evolved through both consistency and adaptation. The initial focus was on fit and performance, with the shoes embracing a more utilitarian look, and New Balance's aesthetic has always been more understated than its competitors, allowing classic silhouettes and thoughtful materials to drive its appeal. However, as the business expanded, so did the approach to design, gradually shifting towards a more sophisticated balance of form and function. New Balance has continued to evolve through the decades, introducing a broader range of colours and designs that showcase the brand's adaptability and relevance to streetwear culture as well as sport.

This evolution has been defined by a series of standout silhouettes. Each of their most iconic models has carried a unique story, being a response to the needs and fashions of its time, whether crafted for dedicated athletes or designed

RIGHT: Model and actress Emily Ratajkowski wearing New Balance 574 in 2023.

ABOVE: New
Balance 320
without N logo.

for streetwear aficionados. From the 990's
revolutionary entry into high-performance running
through to the modern, style-forward 2002R, each
has left an indelible mark.

New Balance 320

The 320 of 1976 was the first shoe to feature the
N logo (see pages 32–37), a time when the company
was transitioning from a modest operation into
a serious competitor in the athletic shoe market,
so the shoe played a crucial role in solidifying the
brand's image.

This shoe was designed with serious runners in
mind, with its superior support system, comprised
of two layers of thick, midsole cushioning. A flocked
nylon upper reinforced with leather resulted in a
lightweight and durable shoe, an achilles pad
added comfort and protection, and the sole brought
excellent traction. Features like these were not

common at the time, and they were intended to produce a shoe that could perform well over long distances. The 320 achieved its goals, being named the number one running shoe on the market by *Runner's World* and described as 'the complete training shoe for the beginning jogger and the Olympic runner alike'.

ABOVE: New Balance 320 with N logo.

New Balance 990

Another cult classic, and seen by many as the ultimate dad shoe, the release of the 990 in 1982 also represented a significant leap forward for athletic footwear. This premium running shoe was the result of four long years of research and development by New Balance's design team, led by a young Steven Smith (see pages 72–74).

The design was ahead of the game in several ways. It was made with materials that were much higher in quality than those traditionally used for running

ABOVE: New
Balance 990v3.

shoes, and it was one of the very first to feature a
suede and mesh upper, which was both breathable
and durable. It featured a 'motion-control device' –
a cushioned footbed that was so successful it's still
used today. It was also equipped with ENCAP
midsole technology (see page 90), blending a
soft EVA core for stability with a sturdy polyurethane
rim for extra stability. This innovation gave runners
an ideal balance between shock absorption
and support.

New Balance wanted to take on its competitors,
and their marketing was appropriately direct, with
a slogan that read, 'On a scale from 1–1000, this
shoe is a 990'. It was promoted as the most
advanced of its kind on the market, but it was
also the most expensive, being the first running shoe

RIGHT: Joe Freshgoods x New Balance 990.

ever to retail for $100 (equivalent to around $325 in 2024). Even Jim Davis had his doubts about this bold move. Looking back in 2013, he recalled, 'At the beginning, when we introduced the 990, it was a real challenge. No one ever thought we'd be able to sell a $100 shoe, but it really surprised us and took off right away. It was a great shoe.'

Even with the hefty price tag, the New Balance 990 quickly gained a reputation for its comfort, stability and style. It became a top choice for serious and casual runners. It wasn't just considered a functional shoe either, having a style that resonated beyond the track, identifying New Balance as a brand that could meet both performance and aesthetic needs. With each new iteration to the series, subtle advancements in technology and style have kept it at the forefront, while staying true to the silhouette that made it a classic in the first place. It stands as a symbol of the New Balance ethos: a dedication to quality, innovation and an aesthetic that resonates across generations.

New Balance 574

Launched in 1988, the 574 delivered the essentials of performance. Like the 990 it was crafted with a durable suede and mesh upper, and featured ENCAP technology for cushioning and stability (see

RIGHT: Basketball player Dwyane Wade wearing New Balance 574 in 2004.

ABOVE: New
Balance 574.

page 90). This gave the shoe a well-balanced
feel, providing enough cushioning for athletic
performance while offering support for casual
wearers who wanted shoes that would feel
comfortable throughout the day. Originally intended
as a reliable running shoe, it therefore quickly
established itself as a comfortable and versatile
silhouette. The 574's understated design also helped.
Among the array of more niche offerings at the time,
the 574 had a universal appeal and it became a
go-to shoe for wide audience. Catering to different
needs and tastes meant that it evolved into one of
New Balance's most enduring designs. Its popularity
has continued for decades and the brand has

capitalized on this popularity by releasing regular updates, allowing its versatility and classic aesthetic to continue to attract new fans.

New Balance 550

Originally released in 1989, the New Balance 550 was designed as a no-frills basketball shoe, purpose-built for performance on the court. It largely remained in the shadows of flashier models from the era and was eventually dropped. But three decades later it was re-released with a fresh vision, and it's now found a prominent place in the world of streetwear. It's said to have been rediscovered by the designer Teddy Santis, who came upon an old image of the shoe, and the new model sneaker was re-released in collaboration with his brand, Aimé Leon Dore. Its simplicity is its charm, with a sturdy leather upper, perforated detailing and a retro-inspired sole that embodies an aesthetic harking back to late 1980s and early 1990s sportswear. New colourways and materials also served to enhance the revived 550 without altering its essential DNA.

BELOW: New Balance 550.

Today's 550 is a seamless blend of past and present – a reimagining that reflects New Balance's ability to evolve its classics, always finding ways to engage both old and new fans.

New Balance 1500

A British-built icon of craftsmanship and style from the Flimby factory (see pages 19–21), and released in the same year as the 550, the New Balance 1500 was an instant favourite, thanks to its streamlined silhouette and careful construction. This model brought a level of sophistication to the New Balance line-up that appealed to those seeking performance without sacrificing style. As had come to be expected from Flimby, the 1500 was built with a combination of premium materials, including suede, leather and mesh, providing durability with a pleasingly lightweight feel. The midsole featured the brand's ENCAP technology (see page 90), and the shoe's sleek, low-profile design gave it the ability to transition effortlessly between performance and casual wear.

The 1500 embodied a balance of function and fashion that few models have managed to achieve, and its reputation for 'Made in UK' craftsmanship and quality has meant that its status has remained. It's a timeless model within New Balance's catalogue.

LEFT: Guest at Milan Fashion Week 2023 wearing New Balance 550.

ABOVE: New Balance 1500.

New Balance 997

When the New Balance 997 stepped onto the scene in 1990, it captured a rare synergy, resonating with both athletes and trendsetters due to its merging of heritage with innovation. Crafted with premium materials, its sleek, refined silhouette embodied a modern aesthetic that still felt effortlessly classic.

Beneath its polished exterior, the 997 introduced New Balance's the latest advanced iteration of its ENCAP midsole technology (see page 90), a true leap forward in running shoe technology at the time.

The 997 had been created as a running shoe, and athletes appreciated its resilience on long-distance treks, yet it also proved comfortable enough to use for daily wear, sparking a new era of performance footwear that could cross over effortlessly into lifestyle wear. The 997's appeal grew as it found its place in street style, and re-releases and

collaborative editions continue to honour the understated elegance of the original.

ABOVE: New Balance 997.

New Balance 998

The New Balance 998 was launched in 1993 and it became a notable addition to the brand's roster, primarily as the first New Balance show to feature its innovative ABZORB cushioning technology (see page 91). This design breakthrough provided an unprecedented level of shock absorption and comfort, especially for runners facing long-distance runs and mixed terrain. The ABZORB midsole was more than simply functional, it marked a shift in how cushioning could blend seamlessly with performance, offering support that felt tailored to each stride.

Beyond its technological edge, the 998's design introduced a refined look that set it apart. With a carefully balanced mix of suede and mesh, the shoe had a visual appeal that reached well beyond the running community. It found a new audience among collectors and fashion enthusiasts, establishing itself as a model with staying power in the ever-evolving sneaker landscape. For footwear enthusiasts, it's become a classic – both a nod to New Balance's commitment to performance and a versatile canvas that continues to inspire reinvention.

New Balance 992

Released in 2006 to commemorate 100 years of being in business, New Balance's 992 was always going to have cultural significance. This much-anticipated American-made shoe featured ABZORB technology in the midsole (see page 91), providing enhanced cushioning and stability, and its design was characterized by a refined aesthetic and premium materials.

The 992's popularity gained perhaps most traction duing the years when Steve Jobs's signature outfit combined a black turtleneck and jeans with a pair of 992s, and it's an association that endures today. Despite this, the 992 wasn't as strong a performer as other models and it didn't remain in production.

RIGHT: Steve Jobs in his signature outfit, including New Balance 992s, in 2007.

ABOVE: New
Balance 1906.

However, the timing of a reintroduction in 2020 was perfectly judged. The impact of this dad shoe classic in a new guise – including a special release designed in collaboration with designer Joe 'Freshgoods' Robinson – was immediate. Although the new 992 was released with minor detailing and technological changes, the shoe retained its crossover visual appeal and it quickly gained a newly iconic status in the contemporary fashion world.

New Balance 1906

Introduced in 2009, the name given to the New Balance 1906 paid homage to the year of the company's founding. It was a throwback, more rugged design that evoked the brand's rich heritage, yet incorporated technology to boost performance and comfort, including N-ergy cushioning for superior shock absorption (see page 93) and the N-lock lacing system for a secure fit.

In 2022, New Balance reintroduced the 1906 model as the 1906R, merging the original upper design with the sole unit of the 860v2. This fusion preserved the shoe's performance capabilities while appealing to contemporary sneaker enthusiasts. The 1906R's popularity was further bolstered by the 1906D model, a distressed suede version conceptualized by in-house designer Yue Wu. In 2024, the 1906U model was released, featuring a rugged design suitable for trail running. This iteration was notably highlighted by a collaboration with Los Angeles-based brand Bricks & Wood, resulting in the 'Echoes of a Butterfly' edition, which showcased a vibrant, nature-inspired aesthetic.

> *The New Balance 1906 paid homage to the year of the company's founding.*

New Balance 2002

The New Balance 2002 was released in 2010. It was designed as a high-performance, luxury running shoe, featuring a leather and mesh upper, and an N-ergy gel sole, but many were put off by its high price tag ($250) and sales were limited.

A decade later, the 2002 was reintroduced as the 2002R, with a refreshed midsole derived from the 860v2. This update retained the original's sleek, nostalgic appeal but retailed for less than most

New Balance footwear, making it accessible to a much wider audience. Its blend of suede and mesh detailing quickly caught the eye of style-conscious wearers, and its popularity was further propelled by limited-edition collaborations with American footwear designer Salehe Bembury and Tokyo-based menswear brand Auralee.

New Balance 327

This modern classic with retro roots debuted in 2020 and paid homage to the brand's heritage by drawing inspiration from 1970s running shoes. Blending retro elements with modern construction, the 327 was immediately recognizable for its oversized N and asymmetrical design. Crafted with lightweight material, it was a fresh look for the brand.

The 327's design featured an angular silhouette, dramatic midsole and textured outsole inspired by trail shoes of the past, while the suede and nylon upper offered the established blend of durability and breathability, giving a level of comfort suited for everyday wear. This approach was carried through to the styling, with attention paid to the details of material and colour palette, producing a shoe that would retain a vintage appeal but would be easily adapted into a fashion-forward wardrobe. Its contemporary yet nostalgic design also appealed to a younger demographic, quickly making it a staple on the streetwear scene. The 327 is a testament to New Balance's ability to blend past inspirations with present-day trends, creating a shoe that appeals across generations.

BELOW: New Balance 327.

Epilogue

As we reach the conclusion of New Balance's storied history – one that has seen it evolve from a small Boston-based firm producing arch supports, into one of the world's leading sportswear brands – it's clear that the brand's legacy goes beyond shoes. And this legacy, in turn, is a testament to its commitment to individuality, craftsmanship, and the fine balance of merging ever-advancing innovation with tradition. It's a unique approach that has won it loyalty among athletes, fashion enthusiasts and everyday wearers.

Rather than following trends, New Balance has created its own, often becoming a symbol of counterculture. And in a world dominated by fast-paced fashion and short-lived partnerships, the brand has crafted a lasting reputation by creating products that resonate on a personal level. Each shoe tells a story; each campaign is intended as a statement of authenticity; each partnership represents a meaningful connection.

The brand's impact will continue to be felt in the world of athletics where it first made its home, but also in the broader landscapes of fashion, music and cultural identity. New Balance has etched its place in history by proving that timeless style and authentic purpose can walk hand in hand, step by step, into the future.

As long as there are stories to be told and distances to be run, New Balance will be there.

Index

Picture Credits

LAURENCE KING

First published in Great Britain in 2025 by
Laurence King
An imprint of Quercus Editions Ltd
Carmelite House
50 Victoria Embankment
London EC4Y 0DZ
An Hachette UK company

The authorised representative in the EEA is
Hachette Ireland, 8 Castlecourt Centre,
Castleknock Road, Castleknock, Dublin 15,
D15 YF6A, Ireland (email: info@hbgi.ie)

A CIP catalogue record for this book is available from the British Library

HB ISBN 9781529444704
Ebook ISBN 9781529444711

10 9 8 7 6 5 4 3 2 1

Cover design and art direction: Luke Bird
Design: Ginny Zeal
Project manager: Victoria Lympus
Printed and bound in Italy by L.E.G.O. S.p.A.

MIX
Paper | Supporting
responsible forestry
FSC® C023419